# CHRISTMAS
## with
## Country Living

Oxmoor
House®

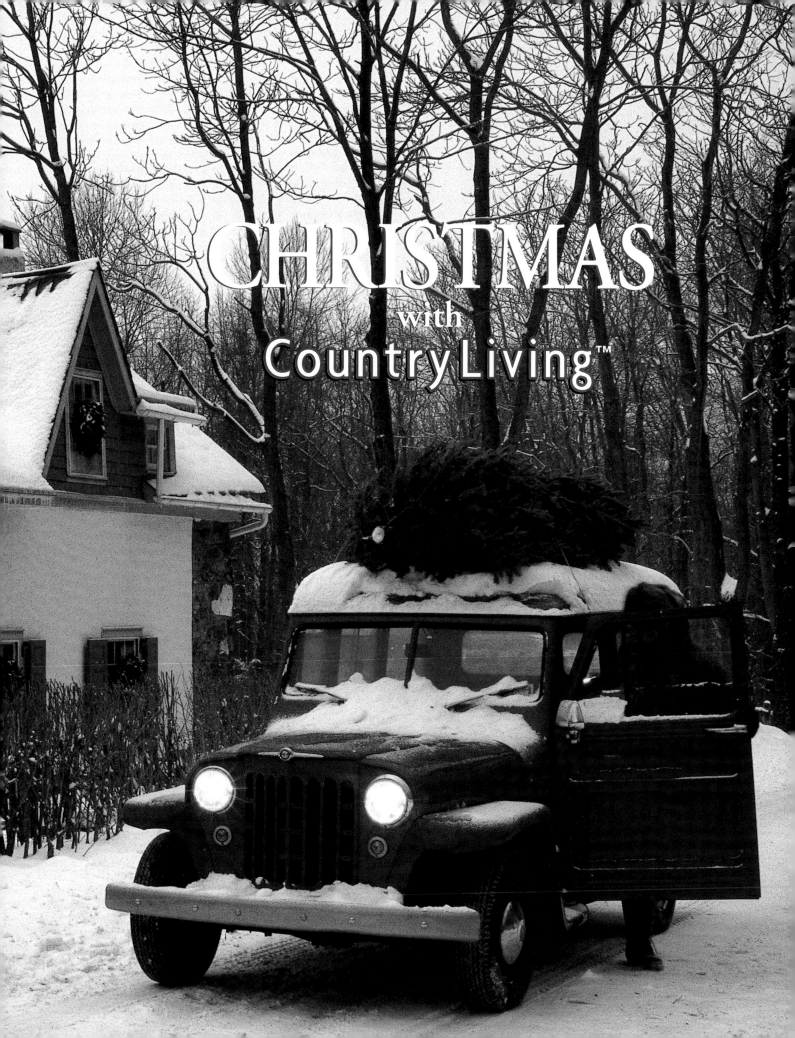

# CHRISTMAS
## with
## Country Living™

*Christmas with Country Living*™
©1998 Hearst Communications Inc., and Oxmoor House, Inc.

*Country Living*™ is a trademark of Hearst Communications Inc.
Oxmoor House, Inc.
Book Division of Southern Progress Corporation
P.O. Box 2463, Birmingham, AL 35201

Library of Congress Catalog Card Number: 97-68505
ISBN: 0-8487-1693-0
ISSN: 1094-2866
Manufactured in the United States of America
First Printing 1998

We're here for you!
We at Oxmoor House are dedicated to serving you with reliable information that expands your imagination and enriches your life. We welcome your comments and suggestions. Please write us at:
Oxmoor House, Inc.
Editor, *Christmas with Country Living*™
2100 Lakeshore Drive
Birmingham, AL 35209
To order additional publications, call 1-205-877-6560.

*Country Living*™
Editor-in-Chief: Rachel Newman
Editor: Nancy Mernit Soriano
Managing Editor: Mary R. Roby
Senior Editor/Decorating & Design: Robin Long Mayer
Senior Editor/Special Projects: Marylou Krajci
Editor/Home Building & Architecture: Pamela Abrahams
Executive Editor/Food: Lucy Wing
Editor/Food: Joanne Lamb Hayes

**Oxmoor House, Inc.**
Editor-in-Chief: Nancy Fitzpatrick Wyatt
Senior Homes Editor: Mary Kay Culpepper
Senior Foods Editor: Susan Payne Stabler
Senior Editor, Editorial Services: Olivia Kindig Wells
Art Director: James Boone

*Christmas with Country Living*™
Editor: Shannon Sexton Jernigan
Guest Editors: Richard Kollath, Edward McCann
Associate Art Director: Cynthia R. Cooper
Senior Designer: Melissa Jones Clark
Editorial Assistant: Cecile Y. Nierodzinski
Copy Editors: Donna Baldone, L. Amanda Owens
Writer: Lola Vickers
Contributing Editor: Janice Krahn Hanby
Illustrator: Kelly Davis
Senior Photographer: Jim Bathie
Director, Production and Distribution: Phillip Lee
Associate Production Manager: Theresa L. Beste
Production Assistant: Faye Porter Bonner

# Contents

# Foreword

Like most of you, we at *Country Living* look forward to the Christmas season, and enjoy the traditions that surround the holiday: unpacking decorations and ornaments; gathering with family, friends, and coworkers; preparing special foods savored just once each year.

It seems the season is upon us earlier than it should be, but Christmas doesn't officially begin until the Christmas tree is chosen—a favorite holiday task. Once the tree is in place, holiday preparations can begin. Before long, the scent of pine begins to mingle with the aroma of paperwhites, pomanders, and freshly baked cookies. They combine to create a sense of well-being and anticipation of seeing loved ones— in short, the undeniable spirit of the holiday.

We've tried to capture that spirit for you here in the pages of *Christmas with Country Living*, with some of our best decorating and craft ideas, as well as a wonderful collection of delicious holiday recipes. This year, we've also added a helpful resource section, which begins on page 156.

Thank you for making *Christmas with Country Living* one of your holiday traditions. All of us at *Country Living* wish you the brightest and best Christmas ever.

The Editors of *Country Living*

# Gathering Trees

The centuries-old tradition of tree decorating symbolizes celebration, renewal, and abundance. Whether a soaring fir or a diminutive tabletop topiary, the Christmas tree is the centerpiece of the holiday home. In town squares and city parks, in formal parlors and casual family rooms, the Christmas tree spreads its generous branches, signaling the return of another season of joy and sharing. Take time throughout the holidays to savor its pleasures.

**Home for the holidays,** the annual tree arrives, signaling the start of the Christmas season (above).

**Christmas trees** wrapped in twine fill the house with the aroma of pine (opposite).

11

False cypress

Each variety of evergreen has its own merits. From the firs that hold their needles well even in the dry heat of a winter home to the aromatic spruce, the soft long-needled pines, and the distinctively shaped cedar, all types will benefit from a little care. Before you leave the lot with a cut tree, ask the salesman to make a fresh cut at the base of the trunk to aid water absorption. Many tree lots will also put the tree in your stand if you bring it with you. Leave the tree outside until you are ready to set it up and keep the well in the stand filled with water. Before you bring the tree inside, position a tree disposal bag on the floor where the tree will go (the bag will be camouflaged by the tree skirt). When Christmas is over, simply lift the bag over the tree to catch any falling needles. Many communities recycle discarded Christmas trees into garden mulch—a fitting way to keep the spirit of the holidays all year!

Fraser fir

Douglas fir

Loblolly pine

White pine

Spruce

**Sculptured evergreens** at Maryland's Ladew Topiary Gardens stand out against a wintry backdrop of bare branches. A fresh snowfall blankets the garden as a distant gazebo stands sentinel over the quiet landscape.

# Wreaths

Christmas customarily begins at the front door with a beautiful wreath embellished with signs of the season, but a wreath's simple and expressive shape makes it welcome anywhere. Try hanging a wreath in every window, propping one on a mantel or a chair, or hanging a small wreath from a shelf. Evergreens and boxwood are the classic materials of choice, but experiment with other mediums as well: strings of dried peppers, hydrangea, lavender, aromatic eucalyptus, and even fresh flowers. Be liberal and creative with material selection. Let the place, the time, and the event be your guide.

A cascade of dried fishtail palm flower plunges from a blushing ring of pepper berries (above). Clusters of yarrow and lavender add unexpected color. Opposite, white tulips and seeded eucalyptus glisten in the shadows of a snowy winter's day. Overleaf: A trio of simple boxwood wreaths underscore a vintage 48-star flag.

# TO CREATE
# A Boxwood Wreath

**1. Purchase** a straw form. For an 18"-diameter wreath, you will need about 40 medium boxwood stems, which are easily trimmed with garden pruners. Anchor green florist's cord to the wreath at one point and knot it to form a loop for hanging. Trim the excess. Tie the cord again at another point on the wreath; do not clip it.

**2. Attach** one bunch of the stems to the wreath top and wrap twine around the stems and the wreath to secure. Continue in this manner until the wreath is thick and full. Knot and clip the twine. To attach a bow, slip a short length of florist's wire through the center knot of the bow. Wrap the wire ends around the wreath and twist them together, concealing the wire in the boxwood.

# Garlands

Generous natural garlands are the ties that bind together the elements of the holiday home. Scented swags of greenery lead the eye inward and upward, frame our favorite views, and underline our favorite vignettes. Versatile garlands can be dressed according to your taste: embellish plain ropes of greens, whether bought or homemade, with clusters of dried flowers, bright berries, pinecones, bows, flags, or cherished ornaments.

**An evergreen swag** is accented with bows and the sparkle of icicles (above).

**Aromatic Fraser fir** and white berries spiral down from the banister to the newel post for a touch that is as dramatic as it is simple (opposite).

**A fragrant** garland circles the room and frames the snowy view. Small tacking nails hold the swag in place, and gilded burlap bows punctuate the points.

**A deep evergreen** swag lends emphasis to a vintage hearth. Polished apples and shiny red berries reflect the ruddy glow of firelight. On the preceding pages, white pine boughs are nestled among natural birds' nests and handmade fabric birds.

# Simple Elements

Small surprises and flights of whimsy add a special rhythm to a holiday setting. Christmas is the time to display favorite collections, to regroup familiar objects so that you see them with a fresh eye. Small gestures—a miniature wreath, a plate of fruit, a handmade doll—arranged in a kitchen cupboard or on a front hall table can have a dramatic impact. Mingle Christmases past and present, color your environment with a touch of wit, and welcome the holidays with open arms.

**A pewter plate** piled with fruit is an invitation to enjoy the abundance of the season (above). Opposite, dried pomegranates align on the edge of a mantel, while a stack of Shaker boxes suggests the outline of a Christmas tree.

31

**Well-loved redware** and a white cylcamen provide a pleasing variation on the holiday's traditional palette (below).

**Casually draped** chiffon ribbon and a dish of green pears are dressing enough for an artfully arranged tablescape (opposite). Miniature wooden lasts, once used to make children's shoes, add a charming bit of sculpture. Overleaf: In a sunny Pennsylvania garden room, a 200-year-old dry sink, still wearing its original blue paint, brims with freshly clipped greens ready for decorating.

**Handstitched birds** nest above a hearth in an arrangement of pine sprigs and pepper berries (above).

**A fabric-lined** sewing basket filled with mending recalls the days of handmade Christmases (top, left). Vintage thread and buttons suggest the crafting of gifts and treasures.

**Faithful friends** keep watch for Christmas: collections of homemade dolls, stuffed animals, and vintage toys are tender reminders of childhoods past (bottom, left).

**The years** may have softened their colors and raveled their edges, but handmade Christmas stockings, embellished with embroidery and bells, hold fresh promise every year (opposite).

**Preserves are displayed** as decoration in an old-fashioned cupboard, along with fresh apples and pine boughs (above). Christmas guests go home with a jar of summer's vegetables.

**Christmas cheer** spills into the kitchen—vintage picnic tins and fine Spode china are pressed into service for a lighthearted holiday setting (opposite).

# Southwestern Style

Winter constellations shine bright in the clear night sky of the Southwest. In many Southwestern towns Christmas begins with the traditional *posada*, a procession that evokes Mary and Joseph's search for a room in Bethlehem. Homes are decorated with colorful hand-painted ornaments and flowering plants, while luminaria shed gentle light along paths and garden walls.

**The branches** of a soaring evergreen are heavy with traditional ornaments and twinkling lights at the Alamo in San Antonio, Texas (opposite). A kitchen door (above) stands hospitably open at Settlers' Crossing, a Fredericksburg, Texas, inn built in 1790.

**A colorful tree** of life teems with playful creatures and hanging fruits (opposite). It looks particularly at home against the weathered layers of a painted plaster wall.

**A traditional earthenware** angel brings tidings of Christmas cheer, as a chorus of smaller angels congregates on a Southwestern windowsill (left).

**Candles** of varying sizes and hues nestle among a cherished collection of Mexican earthenware (below). A small votive shines through the windows of a miniature mission building.

**A ring of chili peppers**—a traditional New Mexico Christmas decoration—offers a spicy alternative to more conventional holiday wreaths (opposite). To make your own, wire clusters of dried peppers to a double-wire frame, varying the angle of the clusters until the frame is full.

**Hand-painted Mexican** clay ornaments (above) and folk-art pieces (below) blend with brightly colored glass balls. The strong colors that characterize Mexican and Southwestern designs are a lively mix of the region's Spanish and native heritages.

# Luminarias

**1. Collect** chunky tapers or pillars with flat bottoms, natural kraft paper sacks, and clean sand. For a neat band, fold the top edge of each sack down 1"; then fold over once more.

**2. Fill a sack** with sand about a quarter full. Place one candle securely in the center of the sand, Repeat with each sack. Arrange them outdoors along a walkway or the party perimeter and light them just before guests arrive.

# Seashore Style

Homecoming has always held a special meaning to those who follow the tides. Villages that teem with tourists during the summer return to their small-town size; beaches and marshes are empty except for a few hardy sea birds. Traditions come with a splash of saltwater: Santa Claus arrives by boat at the head of a floating Christmas parade, lighthouses are hung with giant wreaths and jaunty red bows, and masts and rigging twinkle with tiny white lights. Safe in port, sailors give double thanks for the gifts of the land and the sea.

**A faithful model** of a square-rigged ship sits atop a gilded billet salvaged from a nineteenth-century sailing vessel (above).

**A living** Christmas tree in a dory bobs at anchor just off Nantucket's Easy Street (opposite).

51

**Scallop shells,** starfish, beach glass, and sand dollars are a breezy alternative to more formal tree ornaments. Vintage toy boats hang from the branches; glass balls in several sizes are suspended like glossy pearls. Star ornaments are fashioned from small spiral shells glued togeter with points facing outward.

TO CREATE

# Seashore Ornaments

### 1. Purchase or collect shells,

white cotton twine, and a hot-glue gun. Tie a
small loop of twine and double-knot the ends.
Trim the excess. Hot-glue a twine hanger to the
tip of each shell. For a golden effect, rub on
gold leaf (see page 102 for instructions).

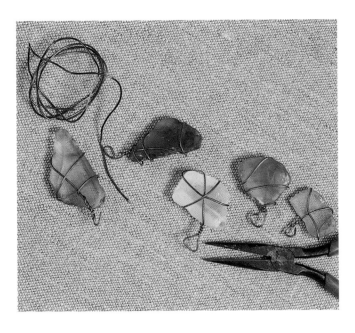

### 2. Smooth beach glass, copper

wire (available from hardware stores), wire
snips, and needlenose pliers combine to make
colorful baubles. For each piece of glass, cut a
10" length of wire, using the snips. Use the pliers to the wrap glass with wire lengths as
shown at left, leaving extra wire at one end for
hanging. Attach the baubles to limbs of
wreaths, trees, or garlands (see pages 54–55
and 56–57).

55

Jewel-like fragments of colored glass sparkle among aromatic bayberry branches in a seaside wreath (left). A wave-tossed bottle wired in place could hold fresh flowers or secret messages.

Washed ashore, an oversize starfish rests on an antique chair (above), making a simple statement of holiday cheer.

# Cabin Style

Time stands still in a snowbound cabin on Christmas Eve. The wind whistles around the corners, the fire crackles in the hearth, and the air is filled with the scent of fresh-cut balsam. Whether your retreat is a log cabin in the woods or an apartment in the city, you can enjoy Christmas cabin style with decorations reminiscent of the unspoiled landscape of the American West.

**Behind the broad** window of a mountain cabin, a lighted Christmas tree twinkles a welcome (above). Stockings stitched from colorful dishcloths hang from the mantel of a Montana cabin (opposite).

**Montana wildlife**——antelope, moose, bear, cougar, and bighorn sheep—circles a simple wreath of greens and berries (above).

**A western ornament** collection shares the tree with a set of whimsical cowboys (opposite). Stuffed animals ride on a wooden train that wraps around the base of the tabletop tree.

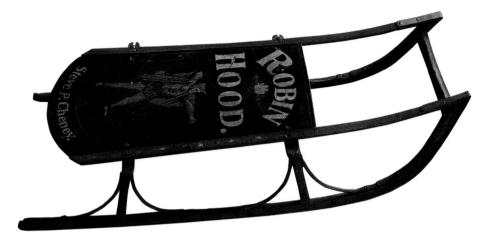

# Sleds

By Lola Vickers

**Who can forget the excitement of speeding downhill on a sturdy sled, taking the bumps belly first and swooshing triumphantly across the straightaway? In a high-tech world, low-tech sleds still offer a matchless thrill that captures the essence of childhood delight.**

Even after they have been retired from active duty, sleds have an irresistible appeal. Often colorful, always sculptural, they evoke the clean, cold days of winter and the uncomplicated joys of snow and speed. Too beautiful to hide in the attic or the barn, a vintage sled can be the centerpiece of a holiday decorating scheme or can be appreciated year-round as a timeless piece of folk art.

Sleds make a charming focal point leaning upright next to a fireplace or on a porch (antique sleds should be displayed in a sheltered environment to protect their paint). A large sled can be used as a coffee table or as a low side table; smaller

62

sleds look striking resting singly on a chest or stacked in a graduated pyramid. Doll sleds, filled with greenery or gifts, make a cheerful holiday centerpiece.

## A Wonderful History—Handcrafted with Care

Sleds were a practical necessity in snowy climates where they were the only means of transportation for many months of the year. Horse-drawn sleighs and ox-drawn sledges carried passengers and large goods, while smaller sleds were used to haul firewood and supplies across the snow. By the mid-nineteenth century, however, children had appropriated the sled for their own use, and gaily colored sleds with sleek runners were being made just for fun.

The first commercial factory devoted exclusively to children's sleds was founded in 1861 by Henry F. Morton of South Paris, Maine. Sleds marked with "Made by Paris Mfg. Co." and a model number or stenciled with the "P/M/C" trademarked logo are still among the most prized by collectors. Paris sleds—the early ones are made entirely of wood, including the runners—were a family affair: Henry's wife, Lucilla, individually hand-painted the decorations on each sled.

Girls followed their brothers down snowy hills but were expected to ride more sedately on special girls' sleds. Boys' sleds—

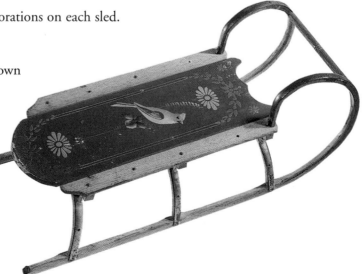

given adventurous names like "Racer" and "Rocket"—were heavier and slung lower for speed, the deck often riding no more than four or six inches above the surface of the snow. Girls' sleds, often decorated with flowers or birds, were lighter, shorter, and smaller, with high runners turned up in decorative curlicues in the front. For as little as 60 cents, a boy or a girl could have a spiffy factory-made sled—the two main types were the cutter, on wide ski-like runners, and the speedier clipper, on slender runners—that would last for a childhood's worth of winters.

## The Famous Flexible Flyer

For generations of children sleds went in only one direction: down. Then on Valentine's Day in 1889, a New Jersey farmer named Samuel L. Allen patented a sled with steering mechanism. The prototype was built from spare parts of farm machinery; Allen called his invention the Flexible Flyer.

From the first the Flexible Flyer, which featured a front yoke that could be pushed back and forth to change the angle of the runners, was a hit. its familiar slatted design and "Eagle" logo remain an icon of childhood. By the turn of the century, the demand for sleds, fueled partly be the popularity of the steering mechanism, was so high that labor-intensive details, such as hand-painted decorations, were jettisoned in favor of mass-produced stenciling.

## Collectors' Treasures

The best place to find old sleds is at antique shows—especially those shows that specialize in toys or folk art—or from antique dealers who carry old toys. It is not unusual to find a good sled priced in the mid- to high hundreds, and the best examples—with hand-painted scenes or motifs, for instance—run in the thousands (although the $60,500 paid at auction by Steven Spielberg for *Citizen Kane*'s "Rosebud" is an exception!)

Any vintage sled will show some wear (in fact, gentle weathering and signs of use can add to its charm), but savvy collectors do take condition into account when they buy. If you are shopping for an old sled, look for one that retains much of its original paint. Decorations may be worn, but they should still be visible; a maker's mark and a date are always pluses, as is any unique mark, such as the owner's name or a special name for the sled. Look at other details as well: some collectors, for instance, value fancy ironwork as much as paint.

Although a single beautiful sled can be a delightful accent in a room or on a porch, there's always room for one more. The fun of hunting through flea markets and antique shops for the perfect old sled can be habit forming—another kind of thrill, without the chill.

**Victorian children** whiled away the long wait for Christmas with holiday games and toys. Clockwise from upper left: a puzzle from Milton Bradley, who began manufacturing such items in 1910; a board game, made at the turn of the century by McLoughlin Brothers in New York; a box of blocks from 1880; a game of Santa visiting homes around the world. Opposite, a classic from McLoughlin Brothers (top); a steeplechase game gets a holiday twist with the addition of Santa and a snowball-throwing elf (bottom). Overleaf: A treasury of vintage ornaments awaits the tree.

# Keepsakes

Tucked away in tissue paper for most of the year, our Christmas keepsakes delight us all over again every time they reappear. Our favorite holiday mementos—old games and toys, glass ornaments, snow domes, nutcrackers, vintage cards, and time-yellowed postcards—become more precious with passing generations. For these most personal of expressions, the only rules of display are the ones that please us most: ornaments can sparkle in a glass bowl, cards can be pinned to a ribbon wall runner, or old toys can sit safely out of reach at the top of the tree.

# Collections

By Lola Vickers

**Every day is Christmas for collectors of holiday decorations and memorabilia. Even in the hottest days of July, you can find collectors poking around flea markets and yard sales, searching for evocative reminders of Christmases past.**

Some collectors hunt by theme—trees, for instance, or snowmen, nut-crackers, or Santas (the German Santa, above, in a cardboard sleigh filled with miniature toys; and the 1910 Santa, opposite, seated on a nodding donkey, are charming examples). Others look for a particular category, such as snow domes, postcards, or traditional Belsnickels, like the ones displayed under a Victorian glass dome (top, opposite). Whatever their specialties, collectors will tell you that the hunt is never over. Like the holiday itself, there's no such thing as too much Christmas.

If you want to start a Christmas collection, begin by looking in your own closets. Even quite recent items can be deemed collectible: strings of colored lights from the 1950s, for instance, sell briskly at flea markets, and bottle-brush trees, some made as recently as the 1960s, have become highly sought after by collectors. Unlike other collectibles, Christmas items need not be in perfect condition to be desirable.

## Origins of the Glass Ornament

Among the most popular collectibles are glass ornaments—everything from simple balls to elaborate and colorful mold-blown shapes. Nineteenth-century German immigrants brought with them the tradition of hanging Kugeln, hollow glass balls silvered with zinc or lead, among the branches of an evergreen. Americans quickly adopted the tradition, and by 1890 Woolworth's alone was importing more than 200,000 glass ornaments from Germany.

Nearly all early blown-glass ornaments came from the small German town of Lauscha, where ornament making became a thriving cottage industry that involved every member of the family, from the father who blew the glass to the small children who carefully fitted the ornaments with metal hangers. By the turn of the century, most glassblowers in Lauscha were using molds, and the number of fanciful designs still to be found is staggering—more than 5,000 by one conservative estimate, including birds, buildings, fruits, vegetables, shoes, and, of course, Santa Clauses, snowmen, and other symbols of the season.

It was only after World War II, when the new border placed Lauscha inside East Germany, that glass ornaments were made in any numbers elsewhere in Europe and eventually in America and Asia. Today, any vintage glass ornament is desirable to collectors, but a good example from Lauscha will always command the highest price.

### The Prized Belsnickel

Many other American Christmas traditions have their roots in Germany as well. Germans settling in Pennsylvania brought with them the Belsnickel, Father Christmas's stern assistant who warned children before Christmas to mend their naughty ways (and who returned on Christmas with a sack full of candy and nuts). In the late nineteenth and early twentieth centuries, papier-mâché and cardboard candy boxes were often molded in the shape of Belsnickel figures and have become highly sought-after collectibles, selling in many cases for several hundred dollars.

Top-dollar Belsnickels, however, are the exception in the world of Christmas collecting. Despite high prices for the rarest and most intricate ornaments and figures, holiday collecting is a highly affordable hobby. Massed together in a single display, even inexpensive items, such as the cotton, cardboard, and papier-mâché snowmen congregated here, make a charming group.

## Caring for Collectibles

Well-loved collections deserve loving care. Fragile glass ornaments should be wired securely to tree branches with florist's wire; as an even safer alterative, they can be individually displayed in wine-glasses set up on a shelf or a mantel. Cards and other delicate paper souvenirs can be hung with clips or tucked into wire racks or mirror frames. To clean ornaments, dust them with a soft artist's brush; never wash with soap and water. Make small repairs promptly and as unobtrusively as possible.

Since many holiday collections spend a good part of the year hibernating, careful storage is important. Avoid extremes of temperature or humidity: hot attics and damp basements are dangerous places for many Christmas collectibles, especially those made of paper or card-board. Each ornament should be wrapped individually in acid-free tissue paper and stored in a sturdy container (specially made boxes with dividers are best—look for them at crafts or Christmas stores).

Although the collection may be packed away, collecting can go on in any season. Happy surprises don't just come wrapped in holiday paper and ribbon—to dedicated collectors, good things come in all sorts of unexpected packages and at all sorts of unexpected times. With the hunt for collectibles, it's easy to enjoy the spirit of Christmas morning year-round.

**The first Christmas card** was created in 1845 by English painter W. C. Dobson, who sent lithographed copies of his work to friends. Seasonal cards and postcards (above) are displayed on a wire rack once used in a retail store. Charming printed Christmas remembrances can still be found for a few dollars at flea markets and antique stores (opposite). Colorful and often highly detailed, they make a lively addition to holiday decorations.

# Candles

Christmas memories are warmed by the remembered glow of candlelight. Carols by the piano, a long Christmas dinner than lingers into evening, the reflection in a child's eyes: there is always room for a few more candles at Christmas. Bring the sight, the scent, and the warmth of candles into your home.

Tuck them into an arrangement of fruit and flowers, encircle the dining table with floor candelabra, arrange columns and tapers in an unused fireplace. You'll light a flame that goes on shining long after the candles have been snuffed out.

A plump beeswax candle mixes its fragrance with the scent of kumquats and limes (above). Overleaf: Tapers illuminate crimson amaryliss blooms.

A tartan bow tethers a bunch of mistletoe to an elegant sconce (opposite).

# Tabletop Trees

Fanciful topiaries bring a touch of magic to the Christmas table. These little trees, surprisingly easy to put together, have a big impact that stays fresh throughout the holiday season. A topiary can be as elaborate as a potted herb, trimmed and trained over months, or as simple as strands of ivy draped over a wire form. And greenery is just the beginning: fruits, nuts, flowers, ribbons, and party favors add charm and color to a tabletop stand of trees.

**Small cookies, kumquats,** and gilded nuts hang from wire topiary forms dressed in ivy and tiny Christmas lights (above). Miniature boxwood topiaries are charming sculptures (opposite). Overleaf: A parterre of potted trees enlivens a dinner setting.

81

# T O   C R E A T E
# A Tabletop Tree

**1. Gather a craft** foam cone (model is a 9"-high cone; add the base container and the stem for the total height), a terra-cotta container, a craft foam block to fill the container, a sturdy wooden branch, a dozen 12" boxwood clippings, and decorator moss.

**2. Break boxwood** trimmings into short stems. Press them into the cone, working from the top to the bottom until the cone is concealed. Press the foam into the container, trimming to fit with a craft knife as necessary. Press the stick into the bottom center of the cone and then into the center of the potted foam. Fill in with boxwood around the base. Glue moss over the foam to finish. Embellish as desired, using floral picks to attach decorations. Hot-glue, wire, or tie a decorative object to a pick and then press it into the foam.

85

# A Grapevine Tree

**1. Begin with grapevine** lengths or a wreath, a cone-shaped wire form in the desired size, garden pruners, wire snips, and heavy-gauge florist's wire. For a 2'-tall cone, you will need two yards of grapevine clusters, each with several stems or two 18" grapevine wreaths. Soak the grapevine in warm water overnight to make it pliable; then remove it from the water. If working with a wreath, clip through the wreath at one point and gently straighten the grapevine into relaxed spirals.

**2. Wrap grapevine spirals** around the cone, beginning at the base, working toward the top, and handling several lengths as one unit. To secure the grapevine, thread wire through the base and tie it around the grapevine. Trim the excess wire with the snips. Continue wrapping and securing with wire until the base is concealed.

# Scents

Nothing stirs deeper memories than our sense of smell. The fragrances of Christmas—the sharp tang of evergreen, the spicy aroma of hot cider, the sweet smoke of a wood fire—connect us with remembered pleasures. By extension, homemade potpourri, sachets, and pomanders bear the gift of memory. By blending your own signature scents, you share old memories and create new ones.

**Aromatic oranges** and limes are etched with a citrus stripper—peels can be saved for garnish or dried for potpourri—and embellished with whole cloves for a strong and spicy scent that is the essence of Christmas. Overleaf: Citrus peel, spices, and dried flowers make pungent potpourri.

# Potpourri

**Dried ribbons** of citrus peel and whole spices—nutmeg, cinnnamon, and cloves—blend into a sweet, musky fragrance. To make three cups of the Citrus Spice blend shown above, combine one cup of broken cinnamon sticks; four whole nutmegs; ½ cup each of star anise, cardamom pods, whole allspice berries; and ½ cup of dried orange, grapefruit, or lemon peel. Add a few drops of essential oil of orange if desired. Mix well. Store in an airtight container for at least one week. Package as gifts or use at home.

**Sharp scents** from a snow-clad winter forest come indoors with a combination of evergreen cuttings and small pinecones. For four cups of the Winter Forest blend at left, combine two cups of pine needles, one cup of miniature pinecones, ½ cup of juniper berries, and ½ cup of rose hips. Add a few drops of essential oil of pine as desired. Mix well. Store in an airtight container for at least one week. For gifts, package in tins or small muslin bags and tie with a holiday ribbon.

**A summer day** recaptured: dried rosebuds and lavender have an old-fashioned fragrance that never goes out of fashion. Replenish dishes of floral potpourri throughout the season with faded blooms from flower arrangements. For three cups of the Lavender Rose blend at right, combine one vanilla bean, one cup of rosebuds or rose petals, one cup of lavender flowers, ½ cup of chamomile flowers, and ½ cup of jasmine flowers. Add a few drops of essential oil of lavender or chamomile as desired. Mix well. Store in an airtight container for at least one week. Package in clear cellophane bags.

# Cake Stands

In the days when dinner was an elaborate affair of many courses, the finale of fruits and sweets was often served on a tiered stand from which diners could pluck their favorites. Today, our tastes may be simpler, but the footed stand has not lost its appeal. A cake stand draws our eye to delightful vignettes that might otherwise be overlooked. Whether a traditional stand of glass, a formal design in silver, or a contemporary interpretation in ceramic or wood, the footed stand raises any presentation to new heights.

A silver cornucopia overflows with chocolates cleverly molded and wrapped to resemble Christmas tree lights (above). Overleaf: Sugared fruit is abundantly heaped on a tiered cake stand.

A 1797 dining room (opposite), includes tiers of flavored jellies, marzipan, and sweetmeats on a double-tiered glass stand.

95

# Sugared Fruits

**1. Coat each piece** of fruit with lightly beaten egg whites, using a pastry brush. Sterilize the brush after using it.

**2. Sprinkle fruits** with granulated sugar and set them aside on wire racks to dry for at least one hour before arranging. Fruits will last about two weeks, but the egg whites make them inedible.

**A doll-sized tree** tops a triple-stacked cake stand that offers polished apples and bright berries (above).

**A tower** of footed stands overflows with green grapes and silver-leafed pears (opposite). For instructions on how to apply silver leaf, turn the page.

T O   C R E A T E

# Gilded Fruits

**1. Purchase gold, silver,** or copper leaf sheets from an art supply store. Gather a paintbrush, scissors, and fresh or artifical fruit. Brush on a thin layer of fixative such as Mod Podge. Let dry until tacky.

**2. Cut a small section of** gold, silver, or copper leaf. Gently press it onto a piece of fruit and peel it off immediately. Repeat to cover each fruit lightly or heavily as desired.

# Handmade Gifts

In our hurry-up world, the loving care of a handmade gift has a meaning that goes far beyond monetary value. Whether it's an expertly stitched set of pillowcases or a paper garland glued together by an enthusiastic child, a gift from the hand is truly a gift from the heart. Imbued with the kind thoughts of its maker, it serves as a precious reminder to slow down and enjoy the passing moment.

**Dried citrus** slices, cinnamon sticks, old lace, and scraps of handmade paper add texture and fragrance to holiday cards (above).

**Let imagination** be your guide when it comes to wrapping gifts. One package (opposite) is wrapped in sheet music blown up on a photocopier.

105

**Old-fashioned pillow** layovers tell a bedtime story. This turn-of-the-century embroidery design reflects everyday life in storybook fashion, the favorite period-style for household linen embellishments. See the instructions on page 149. The patterns begin on page 150.

# Beeswax Ornaments

**1. Melt** 100% pure beeswax or paraffin in an old electric frying pan. (Never melt wax on the stove—it is very flammable.) Oil and chill metal candy or tart molds.

**2. Spoon the** melted wax into molds. To add a hanger, cut 1/16"-wide ribbon to the desired length and fold it in half. With a toothpick, submerge the ends in the hot wax at the top of the mold. Refrigerate.

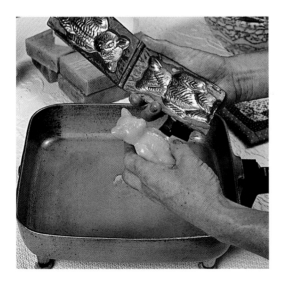

**3. Unmold** when cool. Briefly dip the rim into cool water, rap the back of the mold with a spoon, and invert. Trim the excess wax with a paring knife.

**4. Wash the figures** in soapy water to remove the oil; rinse and dry. Use as place setting favors or ornaments. Store them in a cool, dry place.

**Traditional Danish** woven-paper hearts decorate the tree (above). Their pleasing patchwork pattern is at once graphically modern and charmingly old-fashioned. For instructions on how to make these hearts, see pages 154–155.

**Reindeer** constructed of logs and twigs add a whimsical touch to the lawn (opposite). For instructions to make a tabletop version, turn the page.

# TO CREATE
# A Rustic Reindeer

**1. Gather or purchase** birch twigs and a log (the model was cut from a 3" x 13" piece), a 1" and 2" nail, one 2" flathead screw, a saw, an electric drill, wire cutters and a hammer. Using saw, cut three pieces: one (8") body piece with a 45° angle at one end; one (4") neck piece with a 45° angle at one end; and one (4½") head piece. Cut two (8") pieces from the twigs for antlers, leaving small extensions. Cut four (6½") leg pieces and a 4" tail piece. Drill a starter hole in the neck and the head for nails as shown. Tap nails in with a hammer then use the wire cutters to remove the nail head.

**2. Drill four** ½"-deep holes, using a ⅝" bit for legs on one side of the body section. Repeat to drill two holes at one end of the head section for antlers.

**3. Drill a starter** hole for the screw and then attach the body to the neck. Align the nail with the starter hole and tap the head into place. Tack tail to body with 1" nail. Insert the antlers and the legs.

113

# Simple Touches

Long ago, country families who were snowbound at Christmas and far from city stores learned to make a holiday out of the materials at hand. There's a special delight in assigning new uses for old favorites, whether it's lining a mantel with chandelier prisms, heaping a cradle with pinecones, or filling a humble crate with paperwhites.

**Glittering crystals,** suspended on short lengths of florst's wire, dangle from a garland of fresh ivy (above).

**Stenciled snowflakes** are made by dabbing water-soluble paint over fancy paper doilies onto windowpanes (opposite). The designs come off with the swipe of a sponge when the holiday is over.

# An Ornament Tree

**1. For one glass** tree you will need an 18"-tall craft foam cone; approximately 100 prewired glass floral balls, ranging in size from 1" to 2½" in diameter; a glass or terra-cotta pot to fit the base of the cone; and heavy washers to weight the pot. Fill the pot a quarter full with washers.

**2. Press the** cone into the pot (line a glass pot with foral moss; brush white paint on a terra-cotta pot for a snowy effect). Press the wired end of glass balls into the cone, starting at the bottom and working toward the top. Fill in with small balls as necessary to cover the cone.

**A glossy boxwood** wreath (above) needs no adornment but the discreet sparkle of small silver Christmas balls.

**Cuttings of** long-needled pine tucked into a wooden crate make a pleasingly humble foundation for spires of paperwhite narcissus. At Christmas most garden centers sell bulbs for forcing into bloom.

A plump swag of pine branches is accented with oversize pinecones and dried pomegranates for a simple effect well suited to its early-American setting (above).

The branches of a living evergreen, root-balled for planting after Christmas, are decorated with natural pinecones (opposite). Votive candles line the stairs to light the way to bed on Christmas Eve.

# A Treat for Santa

**By Carol Cook Hagood**

From Mom, I learned at an early age the finer points of leaving treats for Santa Claus. Every family, I know, has its own ways with this time-honored tradition. In households where chocolate chips are a favorite, for example, Santa's treat is likely to be an inviting plate of cookies and milk. Some of Santa's admirers think the best offering is a slice of Christmas fruitcake and a shiny red apple or a cup of hot chocolate meant to chase away the chills.

When I was a child, the treat we left varied every year. Sometimes, we set out a dish of red and yellow fruit-shaped marzipan, fragrant with almond. Sometimes, there was a piece of mile-high divinity, topped with a gaudy cherry. There might be flaky coconut cake or rum balls, rich with festive spirits. But always, the little extra Mom encouraged us to add was some personal communication. It could be a simple handprinted note—Dear Santa, Thank you for your kindness. Merry Christmas!—with the crayon drawing of a Christmas tree. What he'd like best, she'd tell us, is something that we'd made ourselves. And so we folded three-dimensional stars out of colored pages from *National Geographic,* in honor of his worldwide travels, or cut and glued construction paper into tiny wreaths with candles.

As I fell asleep on those long-ago childhood Christmas Eves, among my dreams of dollhouses and paint boxes and shiny skates with keys, I'd spare a thought for Santa on his way. Eyes tightly closed, face pressed into the pillow, I'd see him and his reindeer speeding through a windy night of Christmas stars and moonlit clouds with, far below, the sharp, sweet smell of snow and pine, the darkened shapes of rooftops, the distant house lights. And I'd imagine him later, at our mantel, turning the cinnamon-stick reindeer (or other curiosity I'd made just for him) this way and that in the firelight, smiling with pleasure.

Something extra for Santa. Something surprising; that was the goal. Of course, everyone knew that even if no treats were left, no tasty snack set out to cheer him on his way, no special thank-yous planned, this spirit still would come, laden with treasures. For this was Santa Claus, his heart large enough to hold the wishes of every child in the world. No one could doubt that wonderful gifts were on the way. But the chance to surprise even Santa—to let him know that he, too, was thought of and wished a merry and magical night—that was the something extra that made it nicer. So much nicer.

# Entertaining

**D**oors swing wide in welcome during the holidays, as family and friends visit for long winter evenings of reminiscences and good cheer. Festive food is part of the fun: invite children to help you decorate cookies, polish your silver for a dress-up Christmas dinner, warm carol singers with a spicy punch such as Celebration Wassail (overleaf). Cheers!

**Iced cookie stars** twinkle with brushed-on highlights of liquid silver and several sizes of silver dragées (above). To order handcrafted copper star cookie cutters, see Resources, page 156.

**The fragrant branches** of a blue spruce are decorated with cookie stars and miniature glass balls (opposite). Garlands of beads catch the light of the votive candles on the window sash.

Celebration Wassail

Holiday Eggnog Deluxe

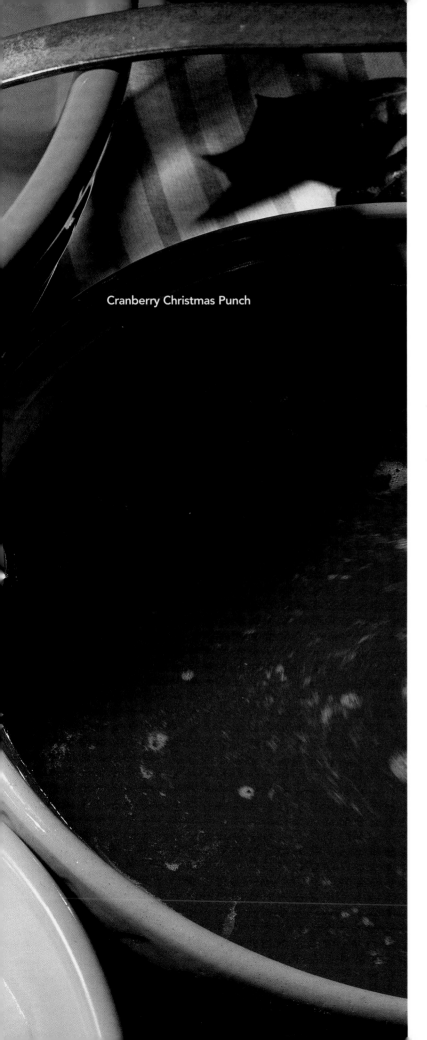

Cranberry Christmas Punch

**Greet holiday guests** with one of these traditional punches. Pour on even more charm with presentations like clove-studded orange slices and freshly ground nutmeg. See page 138 for the recipes.

127

Christmas Cookie Ornaments
Recipes begin on page 140.

**The irresistible smell** of baking lingers even after the cookies are gone. Sugar and spice and everything nice: old-fashioned gingerbread men nestle on a plate with confectioner's sugar-dusted stars. See page 139 for the recipe.

Baked Ham with Madeira Sauce and Browned Potatoes

Holiday Stuffed Goose

Recipes begin on page 142.

Stuffed Crown Roast of Pork

Cornish Game Hens with Cranberry Stuffing

Recipes begin on page 144.

Tennessee Whiskey Glazed Turkey
Stuffed Baked Sweet Potatoes

Green Beans with
Honey-Cashew Sauce

Fresh Corn Spoon Bread

Chocolate Pudding Cake
With Bittersweet Chocolate Sauce

Chocolate Bread Pudding
With Cinnamon Crème Anglaise

Chocolate Macadamia Tart
Recipes start on page 146.

# Recipes

## Christmas Star Cookies

**Makes about twenty 4- to 7- inch cookies.**
**These cookies are intended to be decorations only,**
**and not to be eaten. For edible cookies, prepare**
**Royal Icing with meringue powder rather than egg**
**whites (see note on page 138).**

Shown on pages 124–125

¾ cup sugar
½ cup butter
1 large egg
1 teaspoon vanilla extract
2 cups unsifted all-purpose flour
¼ teaspoon baking powder
¼ teaspoon salt
Royal Icing (recipe follows)
Edible large and small silver dragées (optional)
    (see Note)
Edible liquid silver (optional) (see Note)
White paper plates
Silver thread for hanging

**1.** In a bowl, with electric mixer on medium speed, beat
sugar and butter until light and fluffy. Beat in egg and vanilla
until well mixed. Reduce mixer speed to low. Gradually beat
in flour, baking powder, and salt. Gather dough into a ball,
flatten to a 5-inch round, and wrap in plastic wrap.
Refrigerate dough at least 30 minutes or overnight.
**2.** When dough has chilled, heat oven to 325°F. Lightly
grease two cookie sheets. Cut two
pieces of waxed paper the same size as
cookie sheets. Cut dough round in half.
**3.** Lightly flour waxed paper and roll out half
of dough between paper to ⅛-inch thickness.
Remove top piece of waxed paper from
dough. Using desired star cookie cutter,
cut out as many stars as possible, leaving ½ inch
between each. Remove all trimmings and press together.
Invert waxed paper with stars onto a greased cookie sheet

and peel off waxed paper. Reroll trimmings between floured
waxed paper to cut out more stars. Repeat with remaining
half of cookie dough. If making cookies for hanging ornaments, use a wooden pick to pierce a small (1/16-inch-wide)
hole about ¾ inch from top of one point of each star.
**4.** Bake 10 minutes or until just golden at edges. Cool 5
minutes on cookie sheets; remove to wire racks. Let cool.
**5.** To decorate cookies as pictured on pages 124–125, prepare Royal Icing. Place about ½ cup icing in a pastry bag fitted with a small #1 writing tip; seal and set aside. Beat 2 to 3
tablespoons water into remaining Royal Icing until the consistency of house paint–thick though runny. With pastry
brush, paint the front of cookies with a thick coat of icing
(be sure not to cover up any pierced holes).
**6.** If decorating stars with silver dragées, sprinkle on cookies
while icing is wet; use small dragées to decorate tips of stars
or sprinkle random sizes of dragées for a jeweled effect.
    To achieve a marbled effect, drop dots of liquid silver on
wet icing; drag the tip of a wooden pick through dots and
icing; sprinkle with a few small dragées for added sparkle.
    To paint soft strips of silver on cookies, allow icing to dry
completely. Then, with small artist's brush, lightly brush on
liquid silver, working from the center of cookie outward. If
desired, decorate the center of cookie by applying a large dot
of icing covered with random sizes of dragées.
    To create a 10-point white-and-silver star on top of large
10-point star cookie as pictured on pages 124–125, allow
coat of icing to dry; brush surface lightly with liquid silver.
With a wooden pick, gently scratch in the outline of a
small 10-point star design on top of cook-
ie. With icing in pastry bag, outline small
star. Brush a thin film of icing on the 5 smaller points and in the center of outlined star; cover
with small dragées. With small artist's brush, fill
in outline of larger 5-point star with thinned
icing. Let dry completely. Store in a single
layer in an airtight container.
**7.** Before hanging cookies, to reinforce hole, cut out inch-
long strips from paper plates, trimming them to a width

that's ⅛ inch smaller than the point of the cookie that has the hole in it. Match each strip to point of cookie with hole and mark where the hole is. Remove the strip, and using a hole punch or ice pick, make a hole in the paper strip. Using Royal Icing, glue paper strip to back of star cookie, aligning the holes. Let icing dry. Use silver thread to loop through the hole and paper, then tie together into a knot. Before serving cookies, cut off thread and peel off paper strip.

**Royal Icing:** In a large bowl, with electric mixer on low speed, beat 1 (1-pound) package powdered sugar, 3 large egg whites (if cookies are to be eaten, do not use egg whites; use meringue powder and follow package directions for Royal Icing–see Note below), and ½ teaspoon cream of tartar until mixture is blended. Increase speed to high and beat until very thick and fluffy–about 5 minutes. Cover tightly with plastic wrap to prevent drying until ready to use. Makes 2 cups.

**Note:** Edible dragées, liquid silver, and meringue powder are available from the New York Cake and Baking Distributor, 56 West 22nd Street, New York, NY 10010: 800 942-2539. To order copper cookie cutters see page 156.

## Cranberry Christmas Punch

Shown above and on pages 126–127

1 (3-ounce) package cherry-flavored gelatin
1 cup boiling water
1 (6-ounce) can frozen orange juice concentrate
1 (32-ounce) bottle cranberry juice cocktail, chilled
3 cups cold water
1 (12-ounce) can ginger ale, chilled

**1.** Dissolve gelatin in boiling water. Add orange juice concentrate, stirring until it melts. Stir in cranberry juice cocktail and cold water.
**2.** Gently pour gelatin mixture into a punch bowl. Gently stir in ginger ale. Serve immediately. Yield: 2½ quarts.

## Holiday Eggnog Deluxe

Shown at left and on pages 126–127

6 egg yolks
1 cup sugar
½ teaspoon vanilla extract
¼ teaspoon ground nutmeg
2 cups milk
¾ cup brandy
¼ cup rum
3 cups whipping cream, divided
Ground nutmeg

**1.** Beat egg yolks in a large mixing bowl at medium speed with an electric mixer until thick and pale; gradually add sugar, vanilla, and ¼ teaspoon nutmeg, beating well.
**2.** Place milk in a large heavy saucepan. Gradually add egg yolk mixture; cook over medium-low heat, stirring constantly with a wire whisk, until mixture reaches 160°F (about 30 minutes). Remove from heat; let cool. Stir in brandy, rum, and 1 cup whipping cream. Cover and chill 8 hours.
**3.** When ready to serve, place chilled mixture in a punch bowl. Beat remaining 2 cups whipping cream until soft peaks form. Fold whipped cream into chilled mixture. Sprinkle with additional nutmeg. Yield: 2 quarts.

## Celebration Wassail

Shown at left and on pages 126–127

2 quarts unsweetened pineapple juice
2 quarts apple cider
2 (11.5-ounce) cans apricot nectar
2½ cups orange juice
4 (2-inch) sticks cinnamon
2 teaspoons whole cloves
½ teaspoon ground cardamom
¼ teaspoon salt
Garnish: orange slices studded with whole cloves

**1.** Combine first 8 ingredients in a large Dutch oven; bring to a boil over medium-high heat, stirring occasionally. Reduce heat, and simmer, uncovered, 15 minutes.
**2.** Remove and discard cinnamon sticks and cloves. Garnish, if desired. Serve immediately. Yield: about 5 quarts.

## Sugar and Spice Cookies

Shown below and on pages 130–131

1 cup butter or margarine, softened
1½ cups sugar
1 large egg
2 tablespoons molasses
1 tablespoon water
3¼ cups all-purpose flour
2 teaspoons baking soda
2 teaspoons ground cinnamon
1 teaspoon ground ginger
½ teaspoon ground cloves
Powdered sugar (optional)

**1.** Beat butter at medium speed with an electric mixer until creamy; gradually add 1½ cups sugar, beating mixture well. Add egg, molasses, and water, beating mixture until blended.

**2.** Combine flour and next 4 ingredients; add to butter mixture, beating until blended.

**3.** Divide dough in half. Roll each portion of dough to ⅛-inch thickness on a lightly floured surface. Cut dough with 2- or 3-inch cutters. Place 1 inch apart on lightly greased cookies sheets.

**4.** Bake at 350°F for 6 to 7 minutes. Remove to wire racks to cool.

**5.** Roll edges of cookies in powdered sugar or sprinkle with powdered sugar, if desired. Yield: about 8 dozen.

# Christmas Cookie Ornaments

**Makes about thirty 3½- to 5-inch cookies**
**These cookies are intended to be decorations only, and not to be eaten. For edible cookies, prepare Royal Icing with meringue powder rather than egg whites (see note on page 138).**

Shown at right and on pages 128–129

¾ cup sugar
½ cup butter, softened
1 large egg
1 teaspoon vanilla extract
2 cups unsifted all-purpose flour
¼ teaspoon baking powder
¼ teaspoon salt
Royal Icing (see recipe page 138)
Food coloring (see Note)
Edible gold dragées (optional) (see Note)
Red and green sanding sugar (see Note)
Powdered sugar
Edible green metallic dust (optional) (see Note)
Ribbons and small bells (optional)

**1.** In a bowl, with electric mixer on medium speed, beat ¾ cup sugar and butter until light and fluffy. Beat in egg and vanilla until blended. Reduce mixer speed to low. Gradually beat in flour, baking powder, and salt. Gather dough into a ball, flatten to a 5-inch round, and wrap in plastic wrap. Refrigerate dough at least 30 minutes or overnight.

**2.** When dough has chilled, heat oven to 325°F. Lightly grease two cookie sheets. Cut dough round in half.

**3.** Cut two pieces of waxed paper the same size as cookie sheets. Lightly flour waxed paper; place one sheet on counter, floured side up, then place one half of dough in center and top with other sheet, floured side down. Roll out dough half between paper to ⅛-inch thickness. Remove top piece of waxed paper from dough. Using desired cookie cutters (we used a 3½-inch wreath shape, a 4-inch bell shape, and 5-inch stocking and tree shapes), cut out as many cookies as possible, leaving ½ inch between each. Remove all trimmings and press together. Invert waxed paper with cookies onto greased cookie sheet and peel off waxed paper. Reroll trimmings between floured waxed paper to cut out more shapes. Repeat with remaining half of cookie dough to fill second cookie sheet. If making cookies to use as hanging ornaments, use a wooden pick to pierce a small (1/16-inch-wide) hole about ½ inch from top center of each cookie.

**4.** Bake cookies 10 to 12 minutes or until just golden at edges. Cool cookies 5 minutes on cookie sheets. Remove to wire racks; cool completely.

**5.** To decorate cookies as pictured, prepare Royal Icing. Place ½ cup icing in a pastry bag fitted with a small #1 writing tip; seal and set aside. Divide remaining icing among three small bowls. Tint icing in one bowl pale yellow; tint icing in another green; tint the third bowl of icing red. Beat a few teaspoons water into colored icings until they have the consistency of house paint—thick but runny. Cover each bowl tightly with plastic wrap until ready to use.

**6.** To ice and decorate tree cookies, using a pastry brush, paint the front of cookies with a thick coat of green icing (avoid any pierced holes). Then, dip the tip of a small artist's brush in green food coloring and paint curved stripes of dark green on top of icing to create the effect of branches. Place gold dragées on points of the trees; set aside to dry.

**7.** To ice and decorate stocking cookies, using a pastry brush, paint the bottom two-thirds of the front of each cookie with a thick coat of red icing; sprinkle red sanding sugar over iced part of cookies and set aside to dry. When dry, sift powdered sugar on top third of cookies to create the effect of white trim on stockings.

**8.** To ice and decorate bell cookies, using a pastry brush, paint front of cookies with a thick coat of yellow icing (avoid any pierced holes). While yellow icing is wet, using icing in pastry bag, top yellow icing with loops and swirls of white icing.

Scatter 12 to 14 gold dragées over each bell; let dry.

**9.** To ice and decorate wreath cookies, using a small artist's brush, cover cookies lightly with metallic dust. Using icing in pastry bag, pipe random dots of white icing on wreaths; sprinkle dots with green sanding sugar. When icing on cookies is dry, sprinkle lightly with powdered sugar.

**10.** To store cookies, arrange in a single layer in an airtight container. Do not refrigerate. If cookies are to be displayed only and not eaten, they can be baked and decorated up to one month ahead, though any sprinkling of powdered sugar should not be done beforehand. If cookies are going to be displayed and eaten, prepare and store up to a week ahead, displaying for only a few hours before eating.

**11.** If desired, attach ribbons and bells to hang ornaments.

**Note:** We used Chefmaster's paste food colorings: Forest Green (#7328); Egg Shade (#7326); and Christmas Red (#7374). All food colorings as well as edible dragées, green metallic dust, red and green sanding sugar, and meringue powder are available from the New York Cake and Baking Distributor, 56 West 22nd Street, New York, NY 10010; 800 942-2539.

# Holiday Entrées

Shown below and on pages 132–133

Holiday Stuffed Goose

Baked Ham with Madeira Sauce and Browned Potatoes

Stuffed Crown Roast of Pork

Cornish Game Hens with Cranberry Stuffing

## Holiday Stuffed Goose
**Makes 12 servings**

1 ovenready goose (10 pounds)
Stuffing:
½ pound prunes
3 red apples
2 medium onions, chopped
3 tablespoons butter
½ cup dry red wine
¼ cup water
1 cup fresh breadcrumbs
½ cup walnuts, chopped
3 tablespoons chopped fresh parsley
2 large eggs, beaten
2 tablespoons sugar
1 teaspoon ground cinnamon

**1.** Stuffing—The day before cooking place prunes in a bowl, cover with water; let soak overnight. Drain prunes and remove pits. Chop prunes into small bits. Peel and core 2 apples (reserve 1 for garnish). Chop into small bits. Heat butter in a skillet. Add onions and cook until soft. Remove from heat; add wine and water.

**2.** In a large bowl, combine prunes, apples, breadcrumbs, walnuts, and parsley with onion mixture. Add beaten eggs.

**3.** Goose preparation–Preheat oven to 450°F. Wash goose and dry thoroughly. Stuff goose with the prune mixture. Truss goose. Prick goose all over with trussing needle. Put goose on its side on a rack in a roasting pan. Place pan in oven and cook until goose has browned on all sides. Turn goose often and baste with excess fat.

**4.** Remove goose from oven; reduce temperature to 350°F. Pour off excess fat. Turn goose, breast side up; cook for approximately 2 hours, 30 minutes (or 15 minutes for every pound) or until meat thermometer inserted in thigh registers 180° and in stuffing registers 165°. Pour off excess fat once or twice during cooking.

**5.** To garnish, peel and core remaining apple and slice very thin. Coat apple slices with sugar and cinnamon. Arrange apple slices by overlapping them on breast of goose; brush slices with fat drippings. Return goose to oven and cook 15 more minutes.

**Editor's Note:** Our goose is surrounded by a garnish of red and green apple wedges and fresh mint.

## Baked Ham with Madeira Sauce and Browned Potatoes
**Makes 12 servings**

1 prepared country ham (6 to 7 pounds)
4 carrots, scraped
2 medium onions
3 shallots
2 cups Madeira wine
1¼ cups water
1 clove garlic, crushed
8 potatoes, peeled and each cut in half
1 tablespoon all-purpose flour
2 tablespoons water
Pepper to taste
1 tablespoon unsalted butter

**1.** Preheat oven to 450°F. Remove rind and excess fat from ham. Reserve fat.

**2.** Grate carrots. Slice onions and shallots very thin. Put a few pieces of the reserved fat from ham into a clean casserole and heat until fat is melted. Add vegetables; cook until soft.

**3.** Pour in Madeira wine and 1¼ cups water. Add garlic. Place ham in casserole. Place potato pieces in casserole. Reduce temperature to 350°F. Place casserole in oven and cook ham for 2 hours, turning every 30 minutes so that ham will brown evenly. Baste with sauce in pan. When the bone can be pulled out but still offers some resistance, ham is done.

**4.** Remove ham and potatoes from oven and cover with foil to keep warm. Strain pan drippings into a saucepan over medium heat. Add 1 tablespoon flour dissolved in 2 tablespoons cold water. This will thicken the sauce. Add pepper to taste. Remove sauce from heat and add the butter. Beat well. Serve sauce in a sauceboat with ham and potatoes.

**Editor's Note:** We roasted a regular whole, bone-in ham in a roasting pan rather than a casserole. We served it with the vegetables from the pan and a topping of sautéed onions.

## Stuffed Crown Roast of Pork
**Makes 10 servings**

4½-5  pound crown roast of pork (about 12 ribs)
1  cup peeled, chopped apple
1  cup chopped celery
½  cup chopped onion
¼  cup butter
¾  cup chicken broth
¼  teaspoon ground cinnamon
⅛  teaspoon salt
Dash of ground cloves
Dash of pepper
4  cups fresh ½-inch bread cubes
¼  cup chopped parsley
1  8-ounce package dried apricot halves or peaches, cut up
1  large egg, slightly beaten

**1.** Preheat oven to 350°F. Cover exposed bones on roast with foil to prevent burning during cooking; set aside.

**2.** In large skillet, cook apple, celery, and onion in butter until tender but not browned. Add chicken broth, cinnamon, salt, cloves, and pepper. Cover; simmer over low heat 5 minutes.

**3.** In a large bowl combine bread cubes, parsley, dried fruit, and egg. Pour vegetable mixture over bread mixture, mixing lightly.

**4.** Lightly fill center of roast with some of the stuffing. Place roast on a rack in a roasting pan. Bake 2½ hours or approximately 35 minutes per pound. After 1 hour, cover stuffing in center of roast with foil to prevent burning. Spoon remaining stuffing into a baking dish. Bake stuffing during last hour of roasting pork.

**Editor's Note:** We have added the optional garnishes of fresh apricots and sage.

## Cornish Game Hens with Cranberry Stuffing
**Makes 4 servings**

½  cup chicken broth
1  cup fresh cranberries
3  tablespoons sugar
½  cup chopped celery
⅓  cup chopped onion
½  cup butter
4  Cornish game hens
7  ounces herb stuffing mix
Pepper
Seasoned salt

**1.** To prepare stuffing, bring to a boil in a small saucepan chicken broth, cranberries, and sugar. Reduce heat and simmer, uncovered, 15 minutes or until berries begin to pop.

**2.** Meanwhile, sauté celery and onion in butter. Stir stuffing and cranberry mixture into vegetables.

**3.** Remove and discard giblets from Cornish hens; wash hens and pat dry. Season inside and out with pepper and seasoned salt. Stuff lightly with cranberry stuffing. Spoon any remaining stuffing into an ovenproof casserole dish. Tie legs of hens together securely and dot hens with butter. Bake at 350°F for 1 hour or until meat thermometer inserted in thigh registers 180° and in stuffing registers 165°. After 30 minutes, place dish of stuffing in oven.

**Editor's Note:** We served the Cornish hens on a bed of stuffing with garnishes of cranberries and fresh herbs.

# Elegant Dinner

Shown below and on pages 134–135

Tennessee Whiskey Glazed Turkey

Stuffed Baked Sweet Potatoes

Green Beans with Honey-Cashew Sauce

Fresh Corn Spoon Bread

## Tennessee Whiskey Glazed Turkey
**Makes 12 servings**

1  12-pound fresh or thawed frozen turkey
Quick Onion and Herb Stuffing
    (recipe follows)
3  tablespoons butter or margarine, melted
Giblet Gravy (recipe follows)
½ cup apple jelly
2  tablespoons Tennessee whiskey
2  teaspoons Angostura bitters
Fresh sage sprigs (optional)
Red grapes (optional)
Stuffed Baked Sweet Potatoes
    (optional, page 145)

**1.** Rinse turkey with cold water; drain well. Refrigerate neck and giblets until ready to make broth for gravy. Prepare Quick Onion and Herb Stuffing. Stuff neck cavity; skewer skin to back. Tuck wing tips under shoulder joints.

**2.** Spoon remaining stuffing lightly into body cavity. If opening has a band of skin across it, push drumsticks under it. Otherwise, tie drumsticks securely together with string.

**3.** Heat oven to 325°F. In a shallow roasting pan or dark enamel roaster with lid, place turkey, breast side up, on rack. Brush turkey with 1 tablespoon butter. Insert meat thermometer into center of inside thigh muscle; do not allow thermometer to touch bone.

**4.** If using roasting pan, tear off a piece of heavy-duty foil 2 to 3 inches longer than the turkey. Place foil, tent style, over turkey. Pinch foil lightly at legs to anchor. If using roaster, place lid on top.

**5.** Roast turkey 4½ to 5 hours (or 22 to 26 minutes per pound), basting occasionally with pan drippings, until thermometer registers 185°F or drumstick moves easily. About 45 minutes before turkey is finished, prepare Giblet Gravy.

**6.** To make Tennessee whiskey glaze, in a small saucepan, melt apple jelly over medium heat; stir in whiskey, bitters, and remaining 2 tablespoons butter. Remove foil tent or roaster lid from turkey; brush turkey with glaze. Continue roasting, uncovered, 15 to 20 minutes longer or until skin is browned and shiny. Transfer turkey to a large platter; let rest 15 minutes before slicing. Garnish platter with sage sprigs, grapes, and Stuffed Baked Sweet Potatoes, if desired. Serve with gravy.

**Quick Onion and Herb Stuffing:** In a 6-quart saucepot, combine 1 (10½-ounce) can condensed French onion soup, 1 can water, ¼ cup butter, and 1 cup chopped celery; heat to boiling. Remove from heat and stir in 1 (15-ounce) package seasoned stuffing cubes, 1 large egg, ½ teaspoon dried marjoram leaves, ½ teaspoon dried thyme, and ½ teaspoon dried sage. Use to stuff turkey or transfer to covered 1½-quart casserole dish and bake at 350°F for 45 minutes or until meat thermometer inserted in stuffing registers 165°.

**Giblet Gravy:** About 45 minutes before turkey is finished roasting, in a heavy 2-quart saucepan, sauté reserved giblets and neck, ¼ cup chopped onion, and ¼ cup chopped celery in 1 tablespoon butter until onion is golden. Add 2 cups water, ½ teaspoon salt, and ⅛ teaspoon ground black pepper to mixture in saucepan. Cover pan and heat to boiling; cook over low heat until turkey is cooked. When turkey has been removed from roasting pan, pour drippings from pan into a 4-cup measuring cup. Remove and discard fat from drippings. If necessary, add water to drippings to make 2 cups; return to roasting pan. Remove neck and giblets from broth in saucepan; measure broth and add cool water to make 2 cups. Add 1 cup broth to roasting pan; heat mixture in roasting pan to boiling, stirring to loosen browned-on bits. With wire whisk, stir ½ cup unsifted all-purpose flour into remaining broth until smooth; stir into mixture in roasting pan and cook, stirring until thickened and smooth. Remove meat from neck; chop neck meat and giblets and stir into gravy in roasting pan. Spoon into a sauceboat and serve with turkey.

## Stuffed Baked Sweet Potatoes
**Makes 8 servings**

8  medium-size sweet potatoes
¼  cup orange juice
3  tablespoons butter or margarine, melted
¼  teaspoon ground cinnamon
¼  teaspoon salt
1  teaspoon brown sugar

**1.** Heat oven to 350°F. Rinse and dry sweet potatoes well. Place potatoes on a baking sheet and bake 55 to 60 minutes or until tender. Do not turn off oven. Cool potatoes until easy to handle.
**2.** When potatoes are cool, cut in half lengthwise. With spoon, scoop out pulp from 8 potato halves into a large bowl and discard skins. Scoop out pulp from remaining 8 potato halves, leaving ¼ inch potato intact on skin to make shells. Place pulp in same large bowl; return potato shells to same baking sheet.
**3.** With electric mixer, beat potato pulp, orange juice, 2 tablespoons butter, cinnamon, and salt until smooth. Place potato mixture into a large pastry bag fitted with a star tip; pipe into potato shells, spiraling mixture above shell line.
**4.** Sprinkle remaining 1 tablespoon melted butter and brown sugar over stuffed potatoes. Bake 10 to 15 minutes until potatoes are heated through.

## Green Beans with Honey-Cashew Sauce
**Makes 4 servings**

¼  cup coarsely chopped salted cashews
3  tablespoons unsalted butter
2  tablespoons honey
1  pound green beans, trimmed, cooked tender-crisp, drained

**1.** In large skillet, sauté cashews in butter over low heat until lightly browned–about 5 minutes. Add honey and cook 1 more minute, stirring constantly.
**2.** Pour cashew sauce over beans and toss until coated; spoon into a serving dish and serve immediately.

## Fresh Corn Spoon Bread
**Makes 6 servings**

3  tablespoons butter
3  tablespoons fresh breadcrumbs
3  ears fresh corn, scraped (1½ cups)
⅓  cup yellow cornmeal
½  teaspoon salt
½  teaspoon freshly ground black pepper
2  cups hot milk
1  green onion, finely chopped
   (2 tablespoons)
2  large eggs, separated
2  teaspoons sugar

**1.** Butter bottom and sides of a 1½-quart ovenproof soufflé or deep casserole dish with 1 tablespoon butter; dust lightly with breadcrumbs.
**2.** In a 2-quart saucepan, combine corn, cornmeal, salt, and pepper; stir in hot milk. Cook, stirring constantly, over medium heat, until mixture comes to a boil and thickens.
**3.** In a small skillet, melt remaining 2 tablespoons butter. Add green onion and sauté until just softened–5 minutes. Add onion and butter to cornmeal mixture.
**4.** In a medium bowl, beat egg yolks until light. Stir 2 tablespoons hot cornmeal mixture into yolks; stir yolk mixture into remaining cornmeal mixture until well combined. (The spoon bread may be made ahead to this point, covered, and refrigerated, and carefully reheated to lukewarm before adding egg whites.)
**5.** Heat oven to 325°F. In a medium bowl, combine egg whites and sugar; beat until stiff but not dry. Stir large spoonful of egg whites into cornmeal mixture to lighten it, then fold remaining whites into mixture. Pour spoon bread mixture into prepared dish; place dish inside larger pan and add hot water to a depth of 1 inch. Bake 45 to 60 minutes, or until a knife inserted in center comes out clean. Serve spoon bread immediately.

# Festive Desserts

Shown on page 136

Chocolate Bread Pudding with
Cinnamon Crème Anglaise

Chocolate Pudding Cake with
Bittersweet Chocolate Sauce

Chocolate Macadamia Tarts

## Chocolate Bread Pudding with Cinnamon Crème Anglaise

**Makes 6 servings**

8  ounces bittersweet chocolate or 4 (1-ounce)
    squares semisweet chocolate and 4 (1-ounce)
    squares unsweetened chocolate, coarsely chopped

3  cups half-and-half

1  cup sugar

2  large eggs

4¾  cups fresh breadcrumbs

Cinnamon Crème Anglaise (recipe follows)

2  tablespoons seedless red raspberry preserves
    (optional)

Fresh raspberries (optional)

Fresh mint springs (optional)

**1.** Grease six 3¾-inch individual fluted tube pans (see Note) or 8-ounce timbale molds. In top of a double boiler, over simmering water, melt chocolate. In a 2-quart saucepan, heat half-and-half and ½ cup sugar to boiling.

**2.** In a large bowl, with electric mixer on high speed, beat eggs and remaining ½ cup sugar until thick and lemon-colored. Reduce mixer speed to low; slowly beat in half-and-half mxture. Stir in breadcrumbs and melted chocolate just until combined.

**3.** Heat oven to 400°F. Pour batter into greased pans or molds. Bake 30 to 40 minutes or until centers spring back when gently pressed with fingertip. Prepare Cinnamon Crème Anglaise.

**4.** Cool puddings in pans on a wire rack 10 minutes. Unmold puddings and serve warm or refrigerate and serve cold.

**5.** To serve, pour Cinnamon Crème Anglaise onto each of six dessert plates. Place Chocolate Bread Pudding on Crème Anglaise. If desired, make heart design in Crème Anglaise: Fill pastry bag, fitted with small round writing tip, with melted raspberry preserves. Pipe 6 pairs of preserve dots radiating from pudding. To make hearts, with the tip of a wooden pick, pull a line through each drop of preserves, starting from the side closest to the pudding. If desired, garnish with raspberries and mint.

**Cinnamon Crème Anglaise:** In a 2-quart saucepan, heat 2 cups half-and-half to boiling. Remove from heat. In a large bowl, with whisk, beat 4 large egg yolks and 6 tablespoons sugar. Slowly beat half-and-half into yolk mixture; add 1 vanilla bean, split, 1 (3-inch) stick cinnamon, and ½ teaspoon ground cinnamon. Pour into pan and cook, stirring constantly, over low heat until Crème Anglaise coats a spoon. (Do not boil.) Strain Crème Anglaise into a bowl and refrigerate until ready to serve.

**Note:** We used BUNDT-lettes (or Bundt Muffin) pans from Nordic Ware. They are available wherever baking equipment is sold or may be ordered by calling Nordic Ware's Consumer Service Division at 800 328-4310 ext. 629.

## Chocolate Pudding Cake with Bittersweet Chocolate Sauce
**Makes 16 servings**

Chocolate Cake:
2 tablespoons plus ¾ cup sugar
¾ cup unsifted all-purpose flour
¼ cup unsweetened cocoa powder
¼ teaspoon baking powder
6 large eggs
Pudding:
4 cups whipping cream
10 large egg yolks
¾ cup sugar
1½ cups semisweet chocolate chips
Boiling water
Sauce:
1 cup whipping cream
1½ cups (about 8 ounces) chopped bittersweet
    chocolate
2 tablespoons Grand Marnier or other orange-flavored
    liqueur
White chocolate curls (optional, see Chocolate Curls,
    page 148)
Candied Orange Rind (optional, recipe follows)

**1.** Day before serving, prepare and assemble Chocolate Cake and Pudding. To prepare Chocolate Cake, grease a 10-inch springform pan; sprinkle pan with 2 tablespoons sugar. In a medium bowl, sift together flour, cocoa, and baking powder; set aside.

**2.** Heat oven to 350°F. In a large bowl, with electric mixer on high speed, beat eggs and remaining ¾ cup sugar until double in volume–5 minutes. To prepare batter, gently fold flour mixture into egg mixture just until combined. Pour batter into prepared pan and bake 20 to 25 minutes or until center springs back when gently pressed with fingertip.

**3.** Cool cake in pan on a wire rack 10 minutes. Remove cake from pan and cool completely on wire rack.

**4.** To prepare Pudding, in 2-quart saucepan, heat whipping cream to boiling. In large bowl, with a wire whisk, beat egg yolks and sugar until well combined. Slowly beat hot cream into yolk mixture and pour into saucepan. Cook cream mixture over low heat, stirring constantly, until pudding coats a spoon. (Do not boil.) Remove pudding from heat and stir in chocolate chips until mixture is smooth. Let cool to room temperature.

**5.** To assemble Chocolate Pudding Cake, cut cake horizontally into 3 equal slices. Line inside of cleaned springform pan with foil. Place top layer of cake in bottom of pan. Pour one-third of pudding over cake layer in pan. Top with middle cake layer and half of remaining pudding. Place bottom cake layer, bottom side up, in pan and top with remaining pudding. Cover loosely with plastic wrap and refrigerate overnight.

**6.** Reduce temperature to 300°F. Place springform pan in a large roasting pan; remove plastic wrap. Pour enough boiling water into roasting pan to come halfway up side of springform pan. Bake Chocolate Pudding Cake 1 hour or until top of cake is glazed over.

**7.** Cool cake in pan on a wire rack 15 minutes. Cover loosely and refrigerate until well chilled.

**8.** Just before serving, prepare Sauce: In a 2-quart saucepan, heat whipping cream to boiling. Remove pan from heat and stir in chocolate and Grand Marnier until smooth. Strain sauce and keep warm. If desired, prepare chocolate curls and Candied Orange Rind.

**9.** To serve, remove side of springform pan and slice cake into wedges; place each wedge onto a dessert plate. Top cake wedges with chocolate sauce. If desired, garnish with chocolate curls and Candied Orange Rind.

**Candied Orange Rind:** In a small skillet, heat ½ cup 3- x- ⅛-inch strips orange rind, ½ cup water, and ¼ cup sugar to boiling. Cook 5 minutes or until rind looks glazed. With a slotted spoon, remove rind to a baking sheet to cool.

# Chocolate Macadamia Tarts

**Makes 6 servings**

Shown on page 136

Macadamia Nut Crust:

1½ cups macadamia nuts, finely ground

¾ cup unsifted all-purpose flour

⅓ cup sugar

½ teaspoon ground cinnamon

2 tablespoons butter, melted

Chocolate Filling:

½ cup plus 2 tablespoons heavy cream

3 1-ounce squares semisweet chocolate,
  finely chopped

1 8-ounce package cream cheese, softened

⅓ cup sugar

2 large eggs

2 tablespoons crème de cacao or other
  chocolate-flavored liqueur

Vanilla Sauce (recipe follows)

Chocolate-Dipped Whole Macadamia Nuts
  (optional, recipe follows)

Semisweet chocolate curls (optional, see Chocolate
  Curls)

Powdered sugar (optional)

**1.** Prepare Macadamia Nut Crust: In a medium bowl, combine ground macadamia nuts, flour, sugar, and cinnamon. Stir in melted butter until blended. With fingers, press crust mixture in bottom and up sides of six 4-inch fluted tart pans; set aside.

**2.** Prepare Chocolate Filling: In a 1-quart saucepan, heat ½ cup cream over medium heat. Place chocolate in small bowl. When cream begins to boil, remove from heat; pour over chocolate, stirring constantly until chocolate melts and mixture is smooth; set aside.

**3.** Heat oven to 325°F. In a large bowl, with electric mixer on medium speed, beat cream cheese until smooth. Add sugar and beat 3 minutes. Add eggs, one at a time, beating well after each addition. Beat in remaining 2 tablespoons cream and crème de cacao. Add chocolate mixture; beat just until blended.

**4.** Divide filling among tart shells; bake 25 to 30 minutes or until filling appears set. Cool tarts completely in pans on a wire rack. Cover and refrigerate tarts until ready to serve. Meanwhile, prepare Vanilla Sauce and, if desired, Chocolate-Dipped Whole Macadamia Nuts and Chocolate Curls.

**5.** To serve, spoon some of Vanilla Sauce onto each of six dessert plates. Remove chocolate macadamia tarts from pans and place on top of sauce; garnish top of each tart with chocolate curls and a sprinkling of powdered sugar, if desired. Arrange a ring of 8 chocolate-dipped nuts in sauce around each tart, if desired.

**Vanilla Sauce:** In a 1-quart saucepan, combine ½ cup heavy cream and ⅓ cup milk; cook over medium heat just until bubbles form around edge of pan. Remove from heat. In a medium bowl, beat together 3 tablespoons sugar and 2 large eggs yolks. Gradually pour cream mixture into yolk mixture, stirring constantly. Pour mixture back into saucepan; cook over low heat, stirring constantly, until thickened. (Do not boil.) Strain Vanilla Sauce into bowl; stir in 1 teaspoon vanilla extract. Cover and refrigerate until ready to serve.

**Chocolate-Dipped Whole Macadamia Nuts:** Line a baking sheet with waxed paper. Melt 3 (1-ounce) squares semisweet chocolate in top of a double broiler over simmering water. Dip 1 side of 48 whole macadamia nuts in chocolate; set dipped nuts on lined baking sheet. Refrigerate until chocolate hardens–approximately 15 minutes.

**Chocolate Curls:** Leave block or square of white or semisweet chocolate in a warm place (80° to 85°F) for several hours or heat repeatedly in microwave oven 7 to 8 seconds (just enough to soften chocolate slightly). Place softened square or block against paper towel in one hand; using a sharp vegetable peeler, dig one blade into edge or side of chocolate (depending on how wide you want your curls) and bring peeler toward you; chocolate should come off in curls. If chocolate is too cold it may splinter; if it's too warm it won't curl.

# Handmade Gift Instructions
## Bedtime-Story Pillow Layovers Shown below and on pages 106-107

**Editor's Note:** Each pillow layover is a single layer of fabric, measuring approximately 27½" square plus the width of the lace edging. Make the layover larger or smaller as desired by enlarging or reducing the patterns on pages 150–153. Whichever size you choose, be sure to allow an additional 3¼" all around for the hem.

For our model layovers we used J&P Coats Wound Embroidery Floss, Art C.35; 12 skeins of red # 3500. To make the size shown in the photo, you will need 1 (33½") square of fabric for each layover.

**1. Gather the materials.** You will need a medium-weight closely woven white cotton or linen fabric with an even weave, an embroidery needle, tracing paper, dressmaker's carbon, tape, and a dull pencil.

**2. Prepare the fabric.** Fold the fabric in half lengthwise and widthwise; crease lightly. The intersection of the fold lines marks the center of the fabric. Overcast the fabric edges, if necessary, to prevent raveling.

**3. Transfer the design.** Using tracing paper, carefully trace embroidery pattern (pages 150–153), marking the exact center of the design. Transfer the design to the right side of the fabric, with the center of the design matched to the center of the fabric. Tape the tracing paper to the fabric on four sides. Slip dressmaker's carbon, right side down, between the tracing paper and the fabric. Working on a hard surface and using a dull lead pencil, transfer the design to the fabric. Remove the tape and the tracing paper.

**4. Embroider stitches.** Place the fabric in an embroidery hoop and begin embroidering at the center of the design. Use three strands of six-strand floss throughout.

Embroider all lines in a closely worked stem stitch. For very short lines, such as for eyelashes, use straight stitches. For stitches, refer to the illustraions and the stitching directions below.

**5. Block the fabric.** Wash the fabric in mild detergent. Place it right side down on several layers of clean, dry towels. Let the fabric dry until it is just slightly damp. Steam-press lightly on the wrong side of the fabric.

**6. Hem the layover.** Press the raw edges ½" to the wrong side. Turn each edge 3" to the wrong side, pin in place, and press. Sew the hem in place by hand or machine. About 3" in from each edge, embroider a line of feather stitches from one side edge to the other side edge and from the top to the bottom. Stitch the lace around the edge of the layover as desired.

### Stitching Directions

**Stem stitch:** Working from left to right, take regular, slightly slanting stitches along the line of the design. The thread always emerges on the left side of the previous stitch.

**Straight stitch:** Bring the needle up from the wrong side of the fabric and work single stitches in the desired length and direction.

**Feather stitch:** Work as a series of looped stitches, alternating left to right. Starting on the wrong side of the fabric, bring the needle out. Hold the thread down with the left thumb and insert the needle a little to the right on the same level, taking a small stitch down to the center and keeping the thread under the needle point.

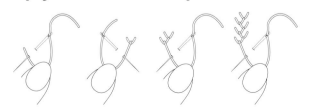

Shown on pages 106–107.
Instructions are on page 149.
For actual size, enlarge 153%.

NING

151

Shown on pages 106–107.
Instructions are on page 149.
For actual size, enlarge 153%.

# Woven Hearts

**Shown at left and on pages 106–107**

**1. Gather the paper.** You will need two pieces of glazed paper, each three times as long as wide and each a different color.

**2. Fold the paper.** Fold each piece in half, with the right side out. From the fold upward, mark a square (Diagram 1). Using the top of the square as the diameter, draw a semicircle above the square with a compass or anything circular, such as a drinking glass (Diagram 2). Cut off the triangular portions and make a cut on each sheet, from the middle of the folded edge up to the top edge of the square (Diagram 3).

**3. Slide the sheets together.** Slide flap X through the paper doubled at O (Diagrams 4–5).

**4. Weave the pattern.** Pull flap X through and gently hook it over the unused flap on the left-hand half of the heart. The other flap is now hooked over the flap marked O and slid between part of the second flap on left-hand half of the heart (Diagram 6). The heart is complete.

**5. Fit with a hanger.** Glue or tape a paper hanger to the back of the heart.

**6. Continue weaving.** For a more complex pattern, cut in from the fold twice, spacing evenly (Diagram 8). Refer to Diagrams 9–10 to connect the sheets. First weave one flap, hook over, in between, and then hook over. For the second flap go in between, hook over, and then in between. The third flap is woven in the same manner as the first.

**7. Vary the weave.** Referring to Diagrams 11–15, you can also change the appearance by cutting four to six even flaps or one wide center flap and two narrow outer flaps.

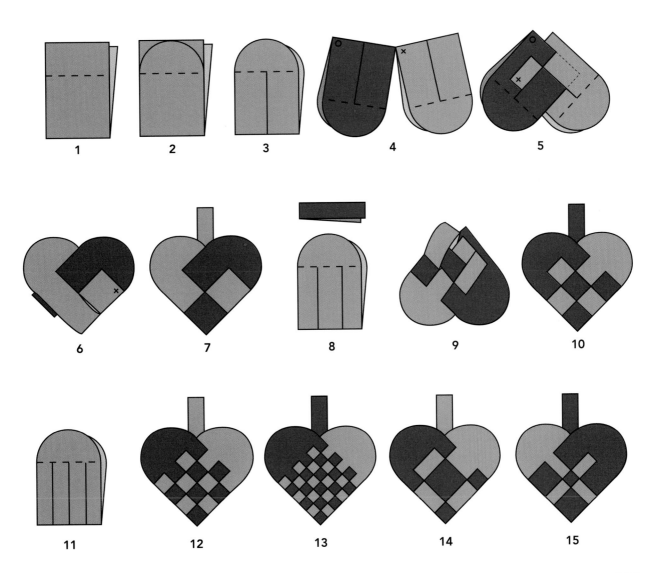

1  2  3  4  5

6  7  8  9  10

11  12  13  14  15

# Resources

Addresses and telephone numbers are subject to change after publication,
as may price and availability of some items.

## Baking Speciality Supplies

**New York Cake & Baking Distributor**
56 West 22nd Street
New York, NY 10010
800-942-2539

**Williams Sonoma**
P.O. Box 7456
San Francisco, CA 94120
800-541-2233

## Beeswax

**Pourette Manufacturing Company**
P.O. Box 15220
Seattle, WA 98115
206-525-4488

## Candles

**Illuminations**
1995 South McDowell Boulevard,
  Building A
Petaluma, CA 94954
800-CANDLES
Call for a free catalog.

**Primavera**
2655-C North Decatur Road, Suite 156
Decatur, GA 30033
404-373-3914

## Copper Cookie Cutters

**Country Living Magazine**
A. Radiating Star 341607 (6")
  $19.95
B. Blazing Star 341604 (6")
  $17.95
C. Star of Le Moyne 341606 (5")
  $17.95
D. 7-Pointed Star 341605 (4")
  $15.95
Set of 4 cutters 341608 $59.80.
Add $3.95 for shipping and han-
dling. Prices valid through January
1999. 800-413-9746

## Decorative Food Molds

**Sweet Celebrations**
7009 Washington Avenue South
Edina, MN 55439
800-328-6722
Fax: 612-943-1688

## Decorative Papers

**Dick Blick Company**
P.O. Box 1267
Galesburg, IL 61401
309-343-6181

**Loose Ends**
3824 River Road North
Keizer, OR 97303
800-390-9979

## Dried Fruits and Flowers

**Hudson & Rose, LTD.**
170 Westphalia Road
Mattituck, NY 11952
516-298-5282

**The Rosemary House**
120 South Market Street
Mechanicsburg, PA 17055
717-697-5111
Send $3.00 for a catalog.

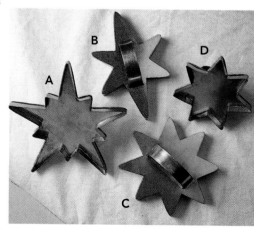

## Dried Herbs

**Sunfeather Natural Soap Company**
1551 State Highway 72
Potsdam, NY 13676
315-265-3648 ext. 22

## Essential Oils

**The Essential Oil Company, Inc.**
P.O. Box 206
Lake Oswego, OR 97034
800-729-5912
Call for a free catalog.

**Lavender Lane**
7337 #1 Roseville Road
Sacramento, CA 95842
916-334-4400

## Eucalyptus

**Tom Thumb Workshops**
14100 Lankford Highway (Route 13)
P.O. Box 357
Mappsville, VA 23407
800-526-6502

## Floral Supplies

**Best Buy Floral Supply**
(Wholesale only)
P.O. Box 1982
  Cedar Rapids, IA 52406
800-553-8497

**Dorothy Biddle Service**
HC 01/Box 900
Greeley, PA 18425
717-226-3239

## Fresh Evergreens
### Garlands/Wreaths/Trees:

**Laurel Springs Christmas Tree Farm**
P.O. Box 85
Laurel Springs, NC
800-851-2345

**Omni Farm**
1369 Calloway Gap Road
West Jefferson, NC 28694
800-873-3327

## Fresh Fruits

**Harry and David Company**
P.O. Box 712
Medford, OR 97501
800-547-3033

## Gift Wrap Supplies

**Caspari**
225 Fifth Avenue
New York, NY 10010
800-CASPARI

**Kate's Paperie**
561 Broadway
New York, NY 10012
212-941-9816

**The Gifted Line**
John Grossman, Inc.
999 Canal Boulevard
Point Richmond, CA 94804
800-5-GIFTED

## Gold Leaf

**Alabama Art Supply**
1006 23rd Street South
Birmingham, AL 35205
800-749-4741

## Pinecones

**Galveston Flower Wreath
Company**
1124 Twenty-fifth Street
Galveston, TX 77550
409-765-8597 or 800-874-8597

## Potpourri

**Sunfeather Natural Soap
   Company**
1551 State Highway 72
Potsdam, NY 13676
315-265-3648 ext. 22

## Reproduction Ornaments

**Margo's Gift Shop**
2058 Yorktown Alley
Tulsa, OK 74114
800-886-2746
Send $15.00 for a catalog.

**Vinny's Showplace**
1076 South Colony Road
Wallingford, CT 06492
203-265-9309 or 800-VINNY

## Ribbon

**Midori**
3524 West Government Way
Seattle, WA 98199
800-659-3049

**Hyman Hendler & Sons**
67 West 38th Street
New York, NY 10018
212-840-8393

**C.M. Offray & Son, Inc.**
Route 24, Box 601
Chester, NJ 07930-0601
908-879-3607

**Impressions/Just Accents, Inc.**
225 Fifth Avenue, Suite 419
New York, NY 10010
212-481-6127

**Grayblock Ribbon Mills**
Saint Michaels Road
P.O. Box 967
Easton, MD 21601
410-822-6100

## Rose Hips

**Tom Thumb Workshops**
14100 Lankford Highway
  (Route 13)
P.O. Box 357
Mappsville, VA 23407
800-526-6502

## Seashells

**Shell Cellar**
South Street Seaport
89 South Street
New York, NY 10038
212-962-1076

## Silver Leaf

**Alabama Art Supply**
1006 23rd Street South
Birmingham, AL 35205
800-749-4741

## Wreath Forms

**Foam/Straw/Grapevine:**
Schrock's International
P.O. Box 538
Bolivar, OH 44612
330-874-3700.
Send $3.00 for catalog.

# Photo Credits

| | | | | | | |
|---|---|---|---|---|---|
| title page | Jeff McNamara | 50 | Carey Hazelgrove | 94 | Steven Mays |
| 2–3 | Keith Scott Morton | 51 | Keith Scott Morton | 95 | Jim Bathie |
| 4–5 | Keith Scott Morton | 52 | Jim Bathie | 96–97 | Keith Scott Morton |
| 6–7 | Keith Scott Morton | 53 | Jim Bathie | 98 | Keith Scott Morton |
| 8 | Keith Scott Morton | 54 | Jim Bathie | 99 | Jim Bathie |
| 9 | Keith Scott Morton | 55 | Jim Bathie | 100 | Jessie Walker |
| 10 | Keith Scott Morton | 56 | Keith Scott Morton | 101 | Paul Kopelow |
| 11 | Keith Scott Morton | 57 | Jim Bathie | 102 | Jim Bathie |
| 12 | Jim Bathie | 58 | Jessie Walker | 103 | Pia Tryde |
| 13 | Jim Bathie | 59 | Jessie Walker | 104 | Polly Wreford |
| 14–15 | Van Chaplin | 60 | Jessie Walker | 105 | Debi Treloar |
| 16 | Keith Scott Morton | 61 | Jessie Walker | 106–107 | Paul Kopelow |
| 17 | Keith Scott Morton | 62 | Jessie Walker | 108 | James Levin |
| 18–19 | Keith Scott Morton | 63 | Jessie Walker | 109 | James Levin |
| 20 | Jim Bathie | 64 | Jessie Walker | 110 | Paul Kopelow |
| 21 | Jim Bathie | 65 | Jessie Walker | 111 | Keith Scott Morton |
| 22 | Keith Scott Morton | 66 | Keith Scott Morton | 112 | Jim Bathie |
| 23 | Keith Scott Morton | 67 | Keith Scott Morton | 113 | Jim Bathie |
| 24–25 | Keith Scott Morton | 68–69 | Peter Margonelli | 114 | Keith Scott Morton |
| 26–27 | Keith Scott Morton | 70 | Jessie Walker | 115 | Debi Treloar |
| 28–29 | Keith Scott Morton | 71 | Jessie Walker | 116 | Paul Kopelow |
| 30 | Keith Scott Morton | 72 | Jessie Walker | 117 | Jim Bathie |
| 31 | Jeff McNamara | 73 | Jessie Walker | 118 | Keith Scott Morton |
| 32–33 | Jeff McNamara | 74 | Jim Bathie | 119 | Paul Kopelow |
| 34 | Steve Budman | 75 | Jessie Walker | 120 | Peter Margonelli |
| 35 | Keith Scott Morton | 76 | James Merrell | 121 | Keith Scott Morton |
| 36–37 | Keith Scott Morton | 77 | Simon Brown | 122 | Keith Scott Morton |
| 38 | Keith Scott Morton | 78–79 | James Merrell | 124 | Keith Scott Morton |
| 39 | Keith Scott Morton | 80 | Paul Kopelow | 125 | Keith Scott Morton |
| 40 | Keith Scott Morton | 81 | Paul Kopelow | 126–127 | Jim Bathie |
| 41 | Keith Scott Morton | 82–83 | Paul Kopelow | 128–129 | Paul Kopelow |
| 42 | Hickey-Robertson | 84 | Kari Haavisto | 130–131 | Jim Bathie |
| 43 | Keith Scott Morton | 85 | Jim Bathie | 132–133 | Richard Jeffery |
| 44 (top) | Keith Scott Morton | 86 | Keith Scott Morton | 134–135 | Richard Jeffery |
| 44 (bottom) | Jim Bathie | 87 (right) | Keith Scott Morton | 136 | Steven Mark Needham |
| 45 | Jim Bathie | 88 | Jim Bathie | 156 | Keith Scott Morton |
| 46 | Keith Scott Morton | 89 | Jean Allsopp | 159 | Keith Scott Morton |
| 47 | Jim Bathie | 90–91 | Debbie Patterson | | |
| 48 | Keith Scott Morton | 92 | John O'Hagan | End sheets courtesy of Nestlenook |
| 49 (right) | Jim Bathie | 93 | John O'Hagan | | Farm, Resort, NH. |